CORAL REEF ECOSYSTEMS

by Tammy Gagne

Content Consultant
Richard B. Aronson, PhD
Department of Biological Sciences
Florida Institute of Technology

Core Library

An Imprint of Abdo Publishing
abdopublishing.com

abdopublishing.com

Published by Abdo Publishing, a division of ABDO, PO Box 398166, Minneapolis, Minnesota 55439. Copyright © 2016 by Abdo Consulting Group, Inc. International copyrights reserved in all countries. No part of this book may be reproduced in any form without written permission from the publisher. Core Library™ is a trademark and logo of Abdo Publishing.

Printed in the United States of America, North Mankato, Minnesota
042015
092015

Cover Photo: Tischenko Irina/Shutterstock Images
Interior Photos: Tischenko Irina/Shutterstock Images, 1; Tina Sotis/Shutterstock Images, 4; iStockphoto, 7, 8 (background), 8 (top), 8 (right), 8 (bottom), 10, 16, 19, 22, 32, 43; Twenty20/Corbis, 8 (top left); Rich Carey/iStockphoto, 8 (middle), 24, 28; John Anderson/iStockphoto, 8 (bottom left); Lars Kirchhoff/iStockphoto, 13, 45; National Oceanic and Atmospheric Administration, 15; Rainer von Brandis/iStockphoto, 21; Howard Chew/iStockphoto, 27; Jodi Jacobson/iStockphoto, 30; NASA, 36; Mary Altaffer/AP Images, 39

Editor: Arnold Ringstad
Series Designer: Becky Daum

Library of Congress Control Number: 2015931040

Cataloging-in-Publication Data
Gagne, Tammy.
 Coral reef ecosystems / Tammy Gagne.
   p. cm. -- (Ecosystems of the world)
Includes bibliographical references and index.
ISBN 978-1-62403-852-5
1. Coral reef ecology--Juvenile literature.   2. Coral reefs--Juvenile literature.
I. Title.
577.7--dc23
                                                    2015931040

CONTENTS

CHAPTER ONE

UNDER THE SEA

ourtney was excited. It was her first time scuba diving in the Florida Keys. This string of islands and coral reefs is off the southern coast of Florida. She had lived in the area most of her life. Still, she had never seen a coral reef up close.

Courtney knew she needed to be careful. Touching the delicate corals could harm them. She also knew not to take anything from the reef.

Scuba diving can be an exciting way to explore coral reefs.

Everything in the reef plays an important role in this ecosystem.

Courtney's diving instructor told her to be watchful. Dangerous animals live among the beautiful corals. A painful jellyfish sting could quickly ruin the day. She hoped to see other marine life, though. Even a short glimpse of a sea turtle would be thrilling.

The Keys are home to about 1,700 species of mollusks and 500 species of fish. With such a variety of life, this amazing ecosystem is as diverse as it is beautiful.

Filled with Life

Combined, the world's reefs cover less than 1 percent of the sea floor. Yet they have a huge amount of biodiversity. This means many kinds of plants and animals live there. One third of the world's ocean fish species spend part of their lives in coral reefs.

What Is a Coral Reef?

A coral reef is an underwater ecosystem. It is made up of plants, fish, and other living things. The organisms of a coral reef live on the hard

The reefs of the Florida Keys are near the shoreline.

skeletons of coral. Corals are tiny animals that live in huge groups, or colonies. The structures they build are known as reefs. Each plant and animal of the reef has a function within the ecosystem.

There are three types of coral reefs. Fringing reefs are the most common. They begin at the fringe, or edge, of a shoreline and extend into the sea. These reefs create a border along coasts. Many fringing reefs are found in the Caribbean Sea.

A Coral Reef Food Web

Many plant and animal species make up a coral reef ecosystem. Each one depends on the other species for its survival. This complex network of living things is called a food web. The arrows show the movement of energy through the web. The sun provides energy for algae and sea grass to grow. Parrot fish feed on both coral and algae. The fish are hunted by lemon sharks. Manatees eat the sea grass.

Barrier reefs also create a border between land and the open ocean. They are much farther from the land than fringing reefs, however. A deep lagoon fills the space between a barrier reef and land. Australia's Great Barrier Reef is one of the world's best-known barrier reefs.

Atoll reefs may have no land near them at all. These reefs formed around volcanic islands. The islands later sank below the water's surface. But the reefs continued to grow upward. Sometimes there is a small piece of exposed land within an atoll coral reef. Wake Island in the Pacific Ocean has an atoll reef.

Corals

Corals are invertebrates. This means they do not have backbones. These tiny animals are related to jellyfish. A single coral is called a polyp. It has a stomach that opens at one end. Its mouth is surrounded by tentacles. The tentacles help the polyp capture smaller animals as food. Tiny creatures called algae live inside corals. The algae turn the sun's light into more food for the corals.

CHAPTER TWO

TROPICAL WONDERS

Most coral reefs are found in the tropical parts of the world. They need warm water to survive. These warm areas are located near Earth's equator. The Caribbean Sea is home to many coral reefs. Reefs can also appear in cooler areas as long as warm currents flow into them. The reefs of Bermuda in the Atlantic Ocean are warmed by tropical currents.

Corals, along with the plants and animals that live around them, require warm water.

The Deepest Reefs

Tropical coral reefs are found as deep as 450 feet (137 m) below the surface. This may sound like a long way down. However, compared to the rest of the ocean, it is shallow. The average depth of the ocean is 14,000 feet (4,267 m).

Some types of coral live in the deep ocean, but they usually do not form reefs. These corals do not rely on sunlight to survive. Instead, they get all the energy they need by trapping and eating nearby organisms. Deep-sea corals have been found as deep as 20,000 feet (6,000 m). This depth makes them harder to study compared to shallow corals.

Depth and Warmth

Water depth plays a key role in coral reef ecosystems. The wildlife in reefs depends on algae. These tiny plants use photosynthesis, the same process that plants on land use to create food for themselves. In this process, the algae take in carbon dioxide and sunlight and give off oxygen and nutrients. These nutrients provide energy for the corals to survive. Deep water can block sunlight, stopping the algae from carrying

The layer of water that receives sunlight is known as the photic zone.

out this process. This means that coral reefs must be in shallow water, usually less than 120 feet (37 m) deep.

In addition to shallow water, life in these ecosystems needs warmth. Coral reef organisms thrive when the water is between 70 and 85 degrees Fahrenheit (21–29°C). They are adapted to survive within this range. Small changes in temperature can harm them. In some cases rising temperatures have even wiped out entire reefs.

Keeping Records

As corals grow, bands appear on their skeletons. These bands give details about the ecosystem's history. For example, the speed that corals grow depends on water temperature. Growth bands can tell scientists how water temperatures have changed over time.

Climate and Weather

The climate in tropical regions is generally pleasant. But storms can be extremely harsh. Hurricanes and smaller tropical storms are common for much of the

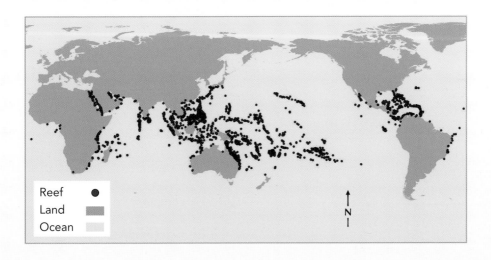

Coral Ecosystems of the World
This map shows where coral ecosystems are located. What can you tell about coral reefs by looking at this map? Where are they most likely to form?

year. Coral reefs serve an important purpose when severe weather strikes. They shield the coastline from the powerful wind and waves.

Storms can help coral reefs. The rushing waters clear out sediment in the reef. This includes dirt and sand left behind by ocean currents. As the sediment washes away, space opens up for more wildlife.

CHAPTER THREE

CORAL REEF PLANTS

Plants help coral reef ecosystems in many ways. Sea grass serves as food for many creatures. Fish, sea turtles, and manatees all eat these plants. Sea grass even helps the ecosystem after it dies. It becomes food for bacteria.

Sea grasses also offer protection to the reef's animals. Predators are less likely to see the helpless young hidden in the grass. The grass does not

Plant life is a critical part of coral reef ecosystems.

guarantee safety, however. Some predators, such as the Caribbean spiny lobster, can move through the grass. They prey on smaller animals there.

Mangroves

Mangroves are trees and shrubs that grow in or near coral reefs. Their dense root systems provide shelter for wildlife. Reefs protect the mangroves from strong ocean waves.

Mangroves also protect reefs. Nutrients enter the water from the shore. The mangroves filter these nutrients from the water. If these nutrients got to the reef, they would cause plant life to grow out of control.

Mangroves and Rainbow Fish

The rainbow parrot fish has a large, beak-like jaw. When it is young, it feeds on plant material it finds near mangroves. Scientists have found parrot fish die off when people remove mangroves from an area.

Mangroves have large, thick roots.

Coral Bleaching

When corals start to lose their algae, their color begins to fade. When the algae leave completely, the corals turn white. This process is known as coral bleaching. One cause of this process is high temperatures. Algae find it harder to survive, and they leave the corals. Another cause is pollution. Runoff from the land can carry pollution to coral reefs. The pollution then harms the algae. Bleaching does not kill corals right away. However, it can put them at risk. In 2005, bleaching caused by high temperatures destroyed about half of the US coral reefs in the Caribbean Sea.

Helping Each Other Survive

One of the most important plants of the coral reef is algae. Seaweed is one of the best-known types of algae. Smaller forms of algae live inside corals. They take in the sun's energy and turn it into food for the corals. They also provide the corals with oxygen and help them remove wastes. The algae benefit too. They use the carbon dioxide the corals produce.

Algae give coral reefs their color. They can make

The bleaching process makes corals appear dull and lifeless.

Corals and algae work together to keep the reef healthy.

the reef look yellowish or brownish. If the algae die, the corals appear white.

Corals, other animals, and plants help each other survive. However, all of these species exist in a careful balance. Coral provides a home for plants and animals. Tiny, single-celled algae provide nutrients to the coral. Larger plants, such as seaweeds, serve as food for animals. Going out of balance can cause damage. Staying in balance is key to a healthy reef ecosystem.

Nancy Knowlton is a coral reef biologist. In an interview, she explained why balance is so important in a coral reef ecosystem:

> Unfortunately, a lot of human activity has a negative impact on reefs. The removal of fish that eat seaweed, for example, is particularly detrimental because the biggest competitors corals have are seaweeds. Seaweeds grow about ten times faster than coral, so in order for a reef to persist, you need things that are constantly eating seaweed—keeping them back like a lawnmower. Parrot fish, for example, act as these lawnmowers, as do various types of sea urchins. If you don't have lawnmowers on the reefs, you effectively wind up with grass.
>
> Source: Margaret Wertheim. "The Reef Builders: An Interview with Nancy Knowlton." Cabinet Magazine. Cabinet Magazine, Summer 2008. Web. Accessed February 26, 2015.

Consider Your Audience

Read this passage closely. How would you adapt it for a different audience? How would you explain coral reef balance to your parents or younger friends? Write a blog post about this passage for a new audience. How does your new approach differ from the original text and why?

CORAL REEF ANIMALS

Among a reef's most valuable animals are fish. Many fish species live in groups called schools. Others spend most of their time alone. Different types of fish have different roles within the coral reef ecosystem. Some act as predators. They keep populations balanced. Others are prey for bigger fish. Many fish are both predators and prey.

Parrot fish feed on corals and algae.

Parrot fish play a unique role in coral reefs. They eat algae, allowing the coral populations to recover when they are damaged. When they feed, they also take little bites of the reef itself. Then the fish expel waste in the form of sand. A single parrot fish can create hundreds of pounds of sand each year.

More Than Just Fish

Octopuses, clams, and snails also live in this diverse environment. They depend on one another for survival. The Caribbean reef octopus feasts mainly on clams and snails.

The giant clam is one of the reef's largest creatures. It can grow to 4 feet (1.2 m) long and weigh 500 pounds (227 kg). It is so big that it cannot move. It stays in the same spot its entire

Unusual Animals

Corals, sponges, and anemones are animals. They look much different from the animals people commonly see. They don't have brains, and they don't move around like most animals. But these creatures have mouths and can digest food. Unlike plants, they cannot produce their own food.

Giant clams can live to be more than 100 years old.

life. For this reason it is often preyed upon by much smaller animals. Eels, snails, and starfish all eat small parts of giant clams.

The giant clam's only protection is its thick shell. Sometimes even this is not enough. Some coral reef snails drill holes in clamshells. These holes allow the snails to reach their prey.

The hawksbill sea turtle was named for its sharp beak.

Working Together

The animals of the coral reef help other organisms in their ecosystem survive. Sea turtles can help coral reef ecosystems simply by eating. The hawksbill sea turtle eats sponges. Sponges compete with corals for space. The green sea turtle eats sea grass. Without turtles, sea grass would grow too tall. It would shade the area below it. The shade would prevent other plants from growing.

Even though they do not move around, sponges can also help. They offer hiding places for other creatures. Tiny fish, shrimp, and crabs all hide within sponges' holes.

Anemones offer clown fish a safe place to lay their eggs. The clown fish protect the anemone from predators such as the butterfly fish. The clown fish also eat parasites that would otherwise harm anemones.

FURTHER EVIDENCE

Chapter Four discusses animals that are part of a coral reef ecosystem. What is the main idea of this chapter? What key evidence supports this idea? Take a look at the website below. Find information from the site that supports the main idea of this chapter. Does the information support an existing piece of evidence in the chapter, or does it add new evidence?

National Geographic: Coral
mycorelibrary.com/coral-reef-ecosystems

CHAPTER FIVE

PEOPLE AND CORAL REEFS

The effects of coral reefs stretch far beyond their tropical ecosystems. Reef fish and other seafood feed more than 30 million people each year. Coral reefs also absorb carbon dioxide in the world's oceans. This gas can affect living things all over the world. Just as the reefs have an impact on humans, the actions of people can help or hurt coral reefs.

Fishers place traps on coral reefs to catch the fish there.

Scuba diving is popular at many of the world's major coral reefs.

Big Business

About 500 million people depend on coral reef ecosystems in some way. Many make their livings from the reefs. Some catch and sell fish and other seafood. Others work in reef tourism.

Coral reefs draw visitors from all over the world each year. People come to see the beautiful corals and amazing wildlife. All of these tourists need places to stay and things to do. Hotels, restaurants, and scuba-diving instructors fulfill these needs. They make a great deal of money in the process. Businesses in the Florida Keys make $1.6 billion each year from coral reefs there.

Tourism can expose the coral reefs to many dangers. People who swim in reef waters may put the plants and animals at risk. Divers and snorkelers can harm corals without even trying. Tourists must learn the right way to treat the reefs and their wildlife.

Pollution

Humans can hurt coral reefs by polluting the water. When trash ends up in the ocean, it can harm reef species. Actions on land can affect coral reefs too. Farmers use chemicals on their crops to help them grow. If the chemicals run into the water, they can cause algae to grow too fast. This can threaten the survival of coral.

Species in Danger

Businesses that rely on coral reefs cannot thrive for long if the reefs suffer. They must respect these natural resources. Overfishing has caused many coral reef species to become endangered.

The prey of the overfished species are also affected. With fewer predators to eat them, these species increase in population. This creates more demand for space and food. All these changes can have harmful, wide-reaching effects on coral reefs.

Overfishing

More than 80 percent of the world's shallow coral reefs are overfished. This means fish are being removed faster than they can grow naturally. If this trend continues, many species could become threatened. Some could even go extinct.

Kelly Heber studies coral reef ecosystems in Indonesia. She explained in an interview how these reefs are in rough shape:

> These reefs suffered during the period from the 1950s to the 1990s, when fishermen commonly exploded cyanide bombs in the water to kill and harvest all the fish in an area at once. Still in recovery, these 'postblast' coral reefs now attract thousands of tourists a year, generating the main source of income for village communities.
>
> To sustain their fragile marine resources, many postblast fishing villages have set up reef-management cooperatives. These self-governing groups of young men establish and live by a set of rules called 'awig-awig,' which guide how the organization leaders resolve disputes with other villages over tour-boat or fishing privileges. They also carry out actions to promote reef health, such as holding dedicated 'reef clean-up days' to pick up after tourists.

Source: Genevieve Wanucha. "Helping Balinese Fishing Communities Build Coral-Reef Management Systems." PhysOrg. PhysOrg, July 3, 2014. Web. Accessed February 26, 2015.

What's the Big Idea?

Take a close look at this passage. What is Heber saying about the coral reefs of Indonesia? Pick out details she uses to make her point.

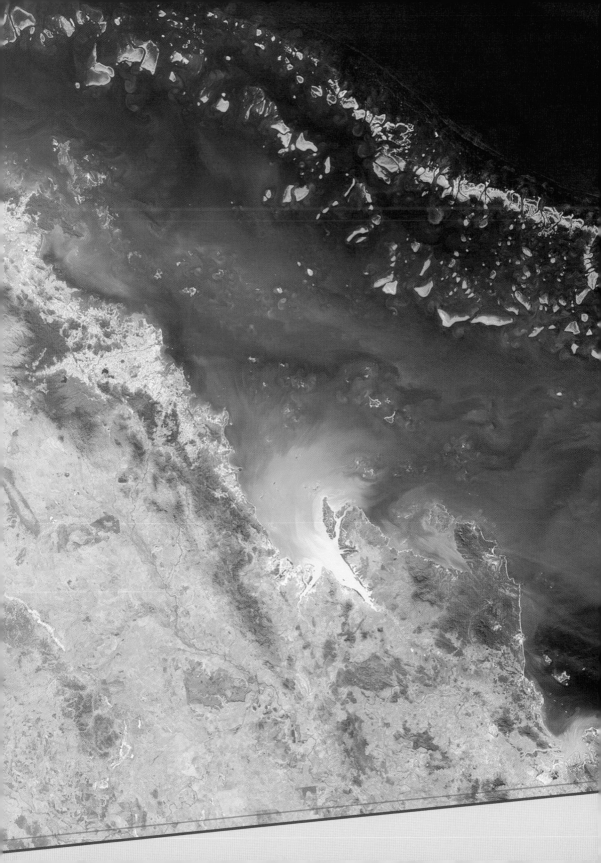

THE FUTURE OF CORAL REEFS

The future of coral reef ecosystems is uncertain. Their fate depends on human actions. People around the world must make coral reefs a priority if these ecosystems are to survive. Poor water quality, rising ocean temperatures, and pollution all threaten our coral reefs.

Australia's fragile Great Barrier Reef can be seen from space.

Carbon Dioxide and Reefs

People and businesses produce massive amounts of carbon dioxide. High levels of carbon dioxide harm reefs in two ways.

First, carbon dioxide is absorbed into the water. While coral reefs use this gas, they can only use so much. The oceans absorb about 1 million tons (907,000 metric tons) of carbon dioxide from the air every hour. This gas changes the water conditions. The change hurts many coral reef plants and animals.

Second, carbon dioxide contributes to climate change. This gas

World Heritage Sites

The United Nations Educational, Scientific, and Cultural Organization (UNESCO) names special places as World Heritage Sites. UNESCO works to protect these important natural or cultural resources. Thirteen World Heritage Sites contain coral reefs. Australia's Great Barrier Reef, the Philippines' Tubbataha Reefs Natural Park, and the Belize Barrier Reserve System have all received this important status.

CHANGING OCEAN
EAN REGULATES
—CHANGING WATER
ANGING CLIMATE

Learning about coral reefs and the dangers they face is
the first step in protecting these amazing ecosystems.

keeps heat trapped in Earth's atmosphere. This causes the average temperature of the planet to rise. The temperature shifts can cause bleaching and harm coral reefs.

Trouble Down Under

Coral reef ecosystems off the coast of Australia have suffered in recent decades. After studying hundreds of reefs in this region, scientists discovered a startling fact. The Great Barrier Reef has lost more than half of its corals in the last 30 years. The scientists named storms and bleaching caused by climate change as the major causes of the loss. Another cause was the population growth of a starfish that feeds on corals. The starfish feed on algae. The scientists blamed their population boom on algae growth caused by runoff from farms.

Protection Needed

Many coral reef species are already suffering. In 2006 the US government named two types of coral as being threatened. They were the elkhorn and staghorn corals. Both grow in the Caribbean. In 2014 the US government named another 22 coral species that need protection. They included pillow corals, three species of star corals, and rough cactus coral.

If climate change continues, some corals could go extinct. To save them, people must reduce carbon dioxide levels. This is the key to saving coral reef ecosystems and their diverse plants and animals.

EXPLORE ONLINE

Chapter Six focuses on the future of coral reef ecosystems. The article below also discusses this issue. As you know, every source is different. How does the chapter present information differently from the article? Why might the two sources present information differently?

A World Without Coral Reefs

mycorelibrary.com/coral-reef-ecosystems

Caribbean Sea

The Caribbean Sea is home to many coral reefs. They are found off the shores of the region's many islands. These include Jamaica, Puerto Rico, and the US Virgin Islands. From a distance the waters are a brilliant turquoise. Up close, though, they are crystal clear.

Florida Keys

The coral reefs off the coast of Florida are known as the Florida Keys. These reefs make up the southernmost part of the continental United States.

Indian Ocean

Some of the Indian Ocean's healthiest reefs are found off the Chagos Islands. The water in this region is extremely clear. This allows more sunlight to pass through, letting corals grow much deeper than they are found elsewhere.

The Great Barrier Reef is extremely vulnerable to the effects of climate change.

The Great Barrier Reef

The Great Barrier Reef is one of the best-known coral reef ecosystems in the world. It is found off the coast of Australia. It is made up of more than 3,000 reefs.

Tell the Tale

Chapter One of this book discusses snorkeling in the Florida Keys. Imagine that you are snorkeling for the first time. Write 200 words about your experience. What plant or animal species might you see? Which would you enjoy seeing the most? Would any animals frighten you?

You Are There

This book discusses how overfishing is threatening coral reefs. Imagine you are a boy or girl living near a coral reef. What if your family made its living by fishing? Would you be worried about the future of the family business?

Surprise Me

Chapter One talks about the fact that corals are animals. This information may have surprised you. After reading this book, what other facts did you find most surprising? Write a few sentences about each one. Why did you find them surprising?

Why Do I Care?

People and businesses that pollute the environment are hurting the world's coral reefs. Why should you care if these ecosystems thrive or struggle to survive? How would their disappearance affect you? What changes could you make to help coral reefs?

GLOSSARY

algae
plants that grow in water and lack stems, roots, and leaves

anemone
a sea animal that looks like a flower and has clusters of brightly colored tentacles around its mouth

extinct
no longer existing

lagoon
an area of water between a coral reef and the shore

manatee
a tropical water-dwelling mammal that eat plants

mollusk
an animal with a soft body that is usually enclosed in a shell containing calcium

parasite
an organism that lives in or on another organism

plankton
a tiny, floating or weakly swimming organism living in a body of water

sediment
material, such as mud and sand, left behind by water or wind

tentacle
a long flexible structure that sticks out, usually around the head or mouth of an animal, and which is used for feeling or grasping

LEARN MORE

Books

Cole, Brandon. *Reef Life: A Guide to Tropical Marine Life.* Ontario, Canada: Firefly Books, 2013.

Gibbons, Gail. *Coral Reefs.* New York: Holiday House Books, 2010.

Simon, Seymour. *Coral Reefs.* New York: Harper Collins, 2013.

Websites

To learn more about Ecosystems of the World, visit **booklinks.abdopublishing.com**. These links are routinely monitored and updated to provide the most current information available.

Visit **mycorelibrary.com** for free additional tools for teachers and students.

INDEX

ABOUT THE AUTHOR

Tammy Gagne has written more than 100 books for adults and children. She resides in northern New England with her husband and son. One of her favorite pastimes is visiting schools to talk to children about the writing process.